Back to the Bleachers

Back to the Bleachers

BASEBALL CARTOONS

STEVE MOORE

Macmillan • USA

MACMILLAN
A Simon & Schuster Macmillan Company
1633 Broadway
New York, NY 10019

Library of Congress Cataloging-in-Publication data available.

ISBN 0-02-860850-X

Printed in the United States of America
10 9 8 7 6 5 4 3 2 1

Book design by Scott Meola

For my sister, Debi, who has always looked after her little brother; and my Grandpa Wilson, who introduced me to the world of Sandy Koufax, Dodger Dogs and the smell of a well-oiled baseball glove.

400

PLEASE
DO NOT FEED
THEIR EGOS

"Stop complaining. First of all, your battling average
has shot up to .450. And second, I warned you about
possible side effects."

"Whoa, whoa, whoa! Excuse me. Step over here and empty your pockets."

"... Wait, wait ... Yes! Sounds like a ground ball! And it's headed this way!!"

The Home Free-Agent Shopping Channel

"Near as I can tell, coach, Fenwick provoked the whole thing. I mean the guy earns 3 million a year and right in front of this woman's seat he quits hustling."

"He says it's nothing personal, but he wants to test free agency and, quote, shop himself around the league, unquote ..."

"Get over here, Bentley! Epstein tore the cover off a baseball, unravelled the string and is about to find out what's at the core!!"

"Anderson, you imbecile! Don't just stand there! ... Throw the ball to the cutoff man!!"

The Ginsu Bat Set

"Hey, wait a minute! Him cheat! This club is packed with cork!!"

"Bean him, Dewey. Not only is he crowding the plate, he's making fun of our uniforms."

Within seconds, Ernie's team of image consultants springs into action mapping out damage control for post-game interviews.

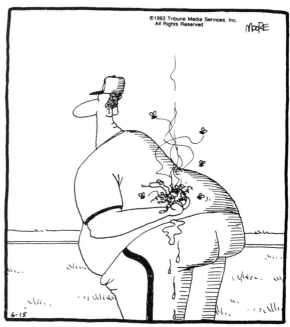

Naturally, the umpires and the opposing teams could never prove a thing. All they knew – when Bernie released the pitch – was that the ball had something extra on it.

When third-base coaches talk in their sleep.

5-27

BULLPEN

" ... We've got two lefties and a right-hander available, coach ... What's that? ... Yeah, yeah. They're loose.''

5-29

At the genuine rawhide baseball ranch

1-900-HECKLE-ME

"Chuck, you fool! Stay back!
Those are rabid sports fans!!"

"Hey, first of all they're actually pretty comfortable, OK?
Second, when a company offers a lucrative endorsement
contract, I don't ask questions."

"Howard's in trouble. Call the bullpen and get us someone with a little more meat on his bones."

Masochist at a batting cage.

Another amusing prank at the home for retired third-basemen.

"Here we go! Another beachball being tossed around. ... Section E. Row 10. ... See it?"

"Yo, coach. Here we go again ... the woman with the heavy breathing."

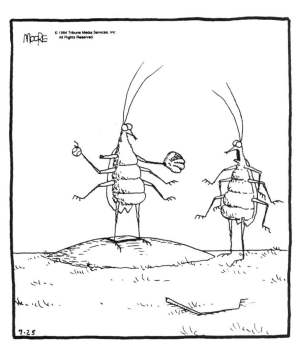

"Well, OK. Keep pitching ... but if you lose another one, I'm taking you out."

"Interesting. So when you swing at a pitch, you're not trying to just meet the ball. You're actually trying to kill it ... Let's talk about that."

"My guess is that he was struck by some kind of small, spherical object. ... Start nosing around. Find out if anyone saw anything."

"Easy, Carl, easy! ... Maybe he intentionally threw at your head to brush you back from the plate, or maybe that pitch just got away from him."

6-10

JAYBIRD HILLS

NUDIST COLONY

"Last night it happened again. Same recurring nightmare.
I'm standing on the mound in Yankee Stadium. Capacity
crowd. Live nationwide TV coverage ... and ... and I'm
completely clothed."

6-7

"OK, what do we have here? ... A missing team mascot,
a pile of costume chicken feathers and a golden
retriever with a dopey grin on its face ... smells like
homicide to me."

29

Coach Yang was torn between an obligation to please the home crowd and a desire to win the game.

"The pitcher's in trouble."

" ... And remember: relaxed stance, back foot planted, level swing ... and don't just try to make contact. Kill it!"

Baseball freaks

33

"Whoa! ... so much for the vow of silence."

"Uh, I gotta go schnookums. Coach needs the phone."

"They go in, they don't come out ... does that bother you?"

Casper and his friends play a game of "over-the-line."

Another ballpark promotional fiasco

" ... Relax, concentrate – and for godsakes ignore the hecklers. First of all, they're just trying to rattle you. And second, it's really not that big."

Umpire with "call waiting."

"Hey, I'm *trying* to throw it over the plate. But I look at his guy and all I hear is a little voice saying: 'Bean him, bean him, bean him ...'"

"Listen, just go up to the plate, get in your stance and stare him straight in the eye. Because if this pitcher senses fear, you're dead meat."

One day at the pitcher's mound

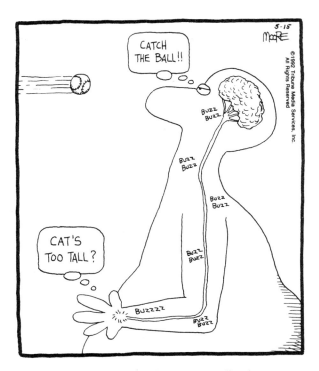

Extremely poor hand-eye coordination

Taken by surprise, Larry gets caught in a rundown between First and Second.

Peanut vendor tryouts

Baseball officials jump on the nationwide "get tough" bandwagon.

Little League chalk talks

"... Fine, thanks. Say, could you do me a big favor? There's a fly ball headed this way. Can you handle it?"

"For crying out loud, Bensen, we can't wait any longer! Get out and walk the rest of the way!!"

In the stadium crowd-control booth

"I don't know, Wayne ... maybe it's just my imagination, but this crowd seems to be getting uglier as the game progresses."

Annual "Schnauzer Giveaway Night"
(Later discontinued)

"Not now, Mike! For god's sake, can't you stall it off for one more inning?!"

"Sorry, Ernie. Time to pull the plug."

"Fool! Get up! You sat on Ted's imaginary teammate!!"

"Head's up!!"

"Inning Five: By spitting, kicking dirt, scratching my rump and imitating other gestures, I have gained begrudging acceptance among these intriguing creatures..."

" ... So then he sticks his glove out and ... Yo, Dave! Was it a 'wicked hop,' a 'nasty hop' or just a regular 'bad hop'?"

How they get batboys

"He originally signed as a left-fielder,
but we're transplanting him to third base."

Gaylord Perry as a kid

At the Hall of Role Models

"... and hereby release us from all liability if struck by a pitch in the head, neck, spleen or other vulnerable part of the body. ... Sign here."

The modern bullpen

"I don't care what you say, that Spitball family is disgusting. Why can't they just wave as they pass by like everyone else?"

"He's been standing in line for an hour ... he thought it was for the restroom."

"Look, I told you at the start of the season:
We win, I treat you to ice cream; we lose, I bring
you here ..."

"Aaaaah!! It's Mike! His career's over and he's
ascending to the broadcast booth!!"

The rise and fall of motor skills: a case study

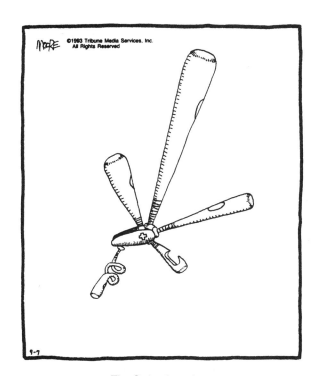

The Swiss Army bat

"Let's give him another five minutes. If he doesn't come to and charge the mound, then I say we go ahead with the bench-clearing brawl without him."

"I dunno, Louie. What do you think? He says they're really good seats ... "

Lonely, cold and frightened, Roger is finally rescued after being left stranded on second base.

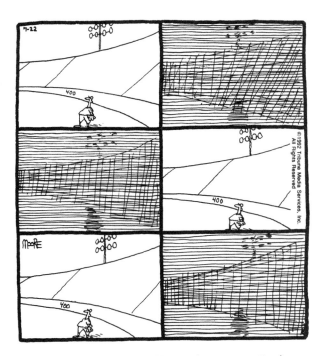

On a dare, Floyd in facilities maintenance attaches "the Clapper" to the stadium light system.

Suddenly, in the bottom of the fifth, the silent killer rose out of deep center field and claimed another victim.

April 21, 1917: The first "Bronx Cheer" is tested.

Longest Line in the Universe Contest

"Hey! Spitwads! Can he *do* that?!"

"... After slaying the dragon, the handsome prince signed a lucrative free-agent contract, his personal life fell into shambles and, inevitably, he entered a substance-abuse treatment program. ... The end."

Baseball, unplugged.

At the Home for Couldabeens

Spring training know-it-alls

"Psssst! Yo, Andy. It's your wife. She's watching the game at home. She says you have a big, gross piece of spinach stuck in your tooth ..."

"He did it! He did it! ... Hand me another hotdog, Helen!"

"Move back!!"

Translating baseball talk

"Bad hop" trolls

72

Why, in sports, you must always yell ''heads up.''

Sensing a confrontation, the umpire steps into the relative safety of the new "Lasorda-proof booth."

Double-play combo in therapy

God is informed of the average annual salary
in major-league baseball.

Velcro walls

"I'll ask you again, coach. Did you or did you not instruct my client to, and I quote, 'Keep your head down' while fielding a ground ball?"

"Hayes! Stop doing that!!"

"Listen carefully, Dewey. Do not – are you listening to me? – do *not* throw the ball until I am *ready* for you to throw the ball."

A screwball pitcher, his knucklehead wife and nitwit kids.

Umpires in hell

"Coach says spread out. ... You're too bunched up."

"He held on to the ball!!"

"Sorry, Ernie. We need to make room on the roster. Someone has to move to the disabled list."

Throughout his major-league career, Darryl was plagued by mental errors.

"The gap in left center field ... and step on it!"

"Forget those three, Coach ...
The one made of straw is prone to mental errors,
the tin guy doesn't have his heart in the game and
the lion is afraid of the ball."

Ernie Terwillinger, Lord of the Bleachers

"Stop! Fools! That's artificial turf!!"

After retirement, Nolan Ryan briefly flirted with a career in show business.

"Curse that woman! She's packed hot dogs again."

"... I'd just released the ball when I heard a 'pop' and I'm like, damn, something's not right here."

Vending fiascos.

Before the invention of catchers, baseball
was a very, very slow game.

"Hey, where's Bob?"

"Well, Bob, you're cured. You may return
to your team now and ... Look out!!"

Steve Moore was born in Denver, Colorado sometime around the time of the signing of the Magna Carta. He grew up in La Canada, California, and was shipped off to college at Oregon State University, which is where he gained most of his knowledge of topsoil and tree lichen.

Naturally, that led to a career in journalism.

Moore has worked for newspapers in Oregon and Maui, Hawaii, as a writer and an editor. He is currently an executive news editor at the *Los Angeles Times*.

Moore was sucked into cartooning under the influence of Gary Larson, B. Kliban and Charles Addams.

Currently, Moore lives in Southern California with his wife, Dru, son, Jakob, and a house full of birds, reptiles and a mentally challenged golden retriever.